MANHATTAN SUITE

An Abstract View of New York

Cv/Visual Arts Research Volume 33

MANHATTAN SUITE
An Abstract View of New York

ISBN 1-904727-12-3
ISSN 1476-9980

A digital format publication from
Cv Publications,
10 Barley Mow Passage, London W4 4PH
tracksdirectory.ision.co.uk

Printed and bound by
Primary Colours Print & Design Ltd
primarycolours.biz

Cv/Visual Arts Research

Formed in 1995 Cv/*Visual Arts Research* is a documentary resource of developments in contemporary art. The survey began in April 1988, and was first published as the quarterly review *Cv Journal of Art and Crafts* (later *Cv Journal of the Arts)*. *Cv* was produced until 1992 and the collection of interviews, features and reviews provided the basis of the Cv/*VAR* archive and subsequent publications. Cv/*VAR* addresses the fields of academic research and a growing non-specialist readership. The archive is categorized as *Interviews - Artists; Curators & Collections; Crafts Directory; Small Histories; Social Studies* and *Studio Work* . Titles are published as books and monographs, with   CDs and DVDs in the software catalogue.

Cv/VAR series no.33 documents eighty panel paintings made in December 2003. The 30cm square studies take locations of Manhattan to develop an abstract interpretation of the city. Vivid colour chords of lilac, red, lemon and black, are orchestrated in a dynamic textured range, evoking the energy and vivacity of the city. The book includes photographs and notes from visits made between 1976 and 1998.

The Author:

Nicholas Wegner. *Born* 1948, Bromley, Kent, England. *Studied* Painting with Frank Auerbach and Keith Vaughan at the Slade School, UCL (BA); Printmaking with Stanley Jones at The Curwen Press and History of Art (MA) Kingston University. Operated The Gallery, 65a Lisson Street 1973-78, working with Vaughan Grylls, 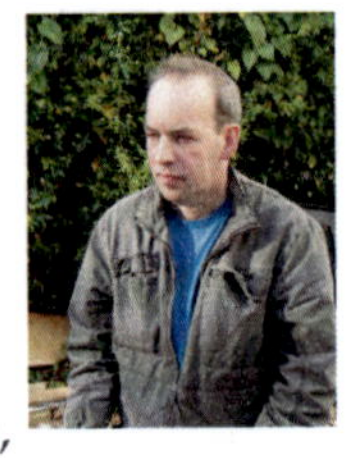 John Latham, Rita Donagh and others. *Freelance and Editorial:* Reviews and features for What's On In London, Artists Newsletter, Art Monthly, The Artist and Artslant.com. 1994-95 House writer for The Dictionary of Art (Macmillan London & New York) contributing over eighty entries. With Anna Douglas compiled Artists Stories (AN Publications 1996). With Sarah Batiste edited and published Cv Journal of Art and Crafts 1988-91, forming Cv Publications in 1992 and Cv/Visual Arts Research in 1995.

CONTENTS

  May 1976 George Washington Hotel . Lobby . Sidewalk . Transfers . Dime Store . Time Square . Andy Studio . Guggenheim . Geldzahler . Museum Store . Artforum . Bus Stop . Party in the upper 80s . 1979 The Prince George Hotel . Harlem . The Bronx . Charades . 1998 . Marriot Hotel, Time Square.

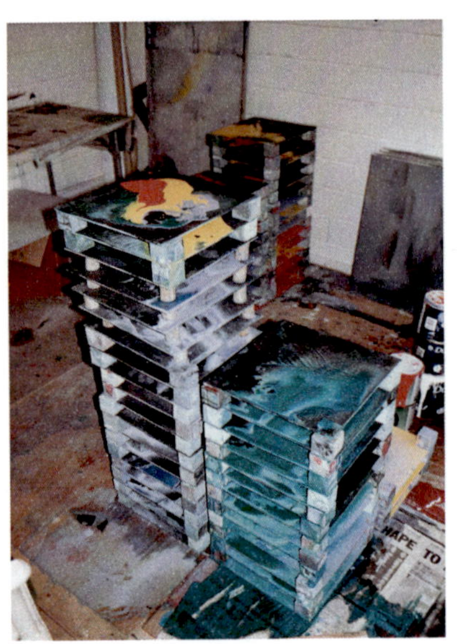

Manhattan Stack
04/ 2003

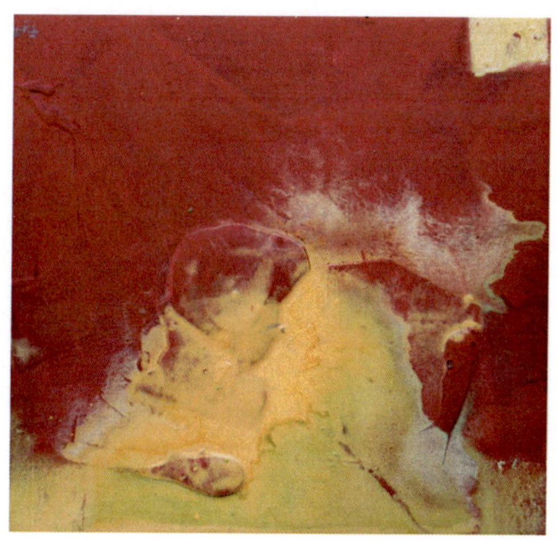

Allen Street
Emulsion on panel 12 x 12″
(30 x 30cms)

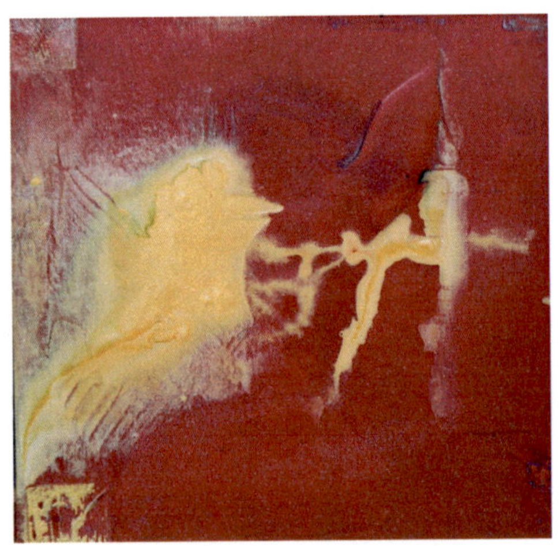

Amsterdam
Emulsion on panel 12 x 12″
(30 x 30cms)

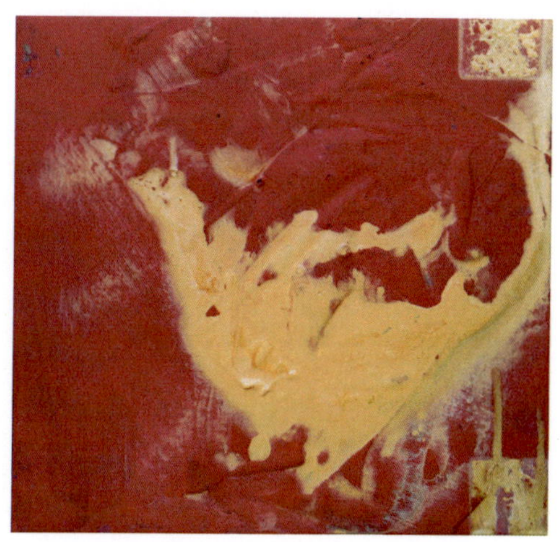

Astoria
Emulsion on panel 12 x 12"
(30 x 30cms)

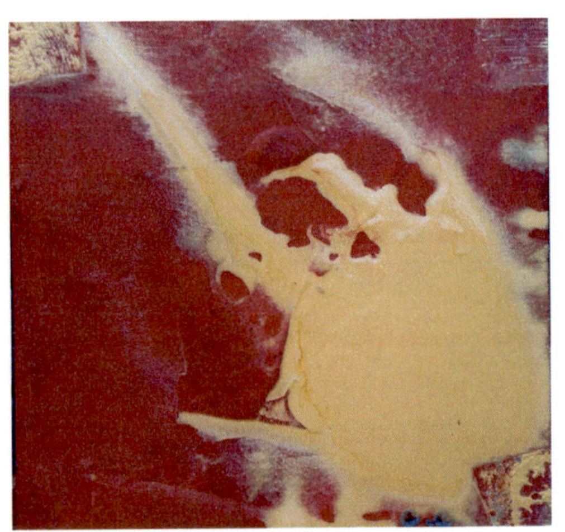

Audubon Avenue
Emulsion on panel 12 x 12″
(30 x 30cms)

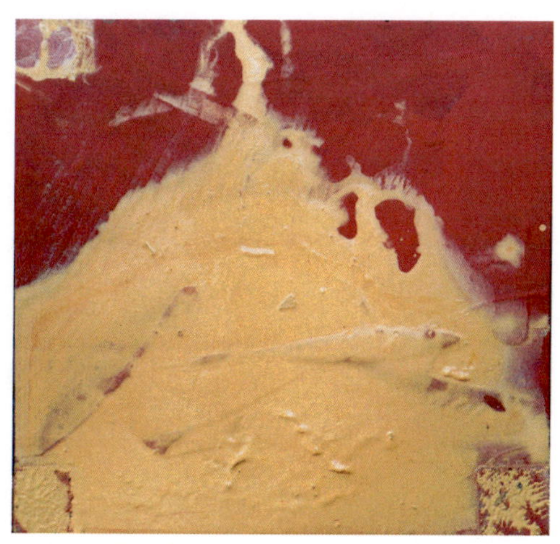

Avenue Of The Americas
Emulsion on panel 12 x 12″
(30 x 30cms)

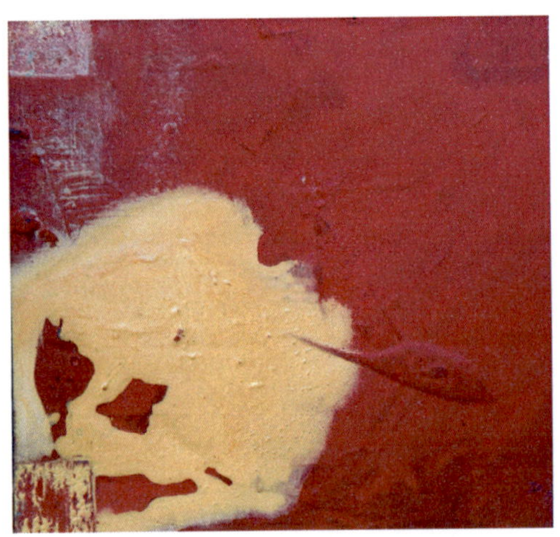

Battery Park
Emulsion on panel 12 x 12"
(30 x 30cms)

13

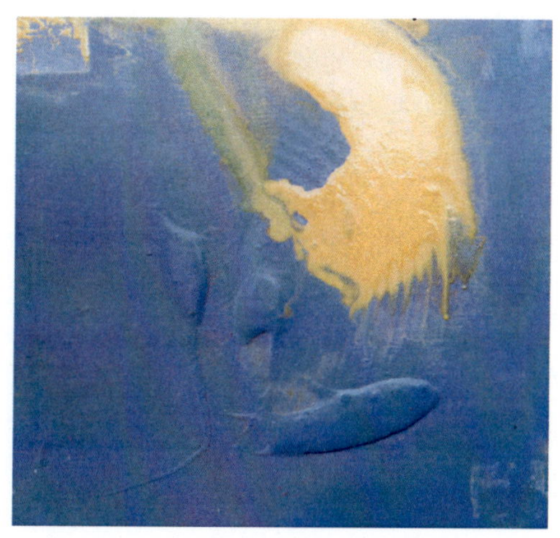

Bleeker Street
Emulsion on panel 12 x 12″
(30 x 30cms)

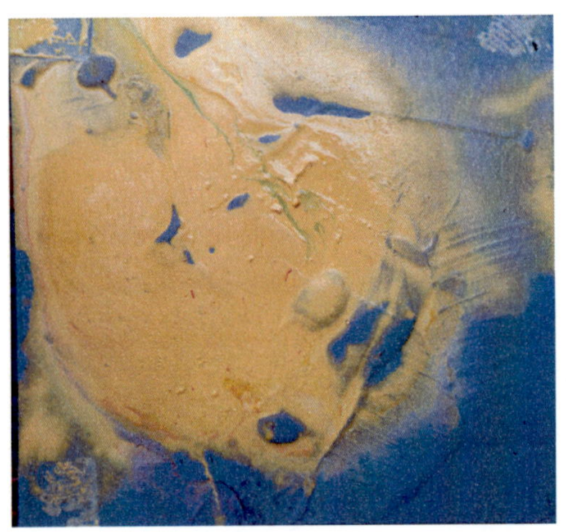

Bowling Green
Emulsion on panel 12 x 12″
(30 x 30cms)

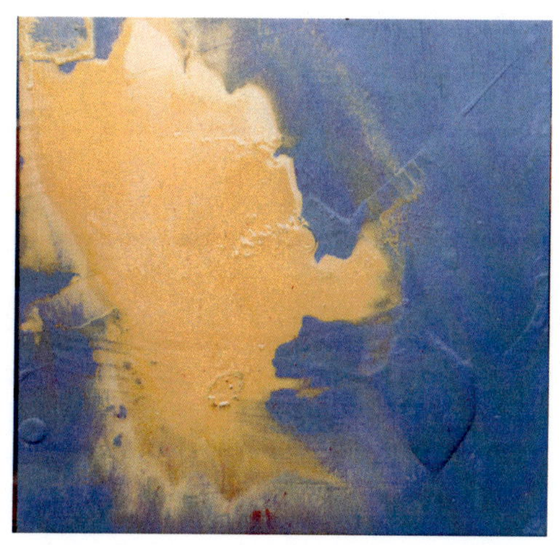

Broad Street
Emulsion on panel 12 x 12"
(30 x 30cms)

16

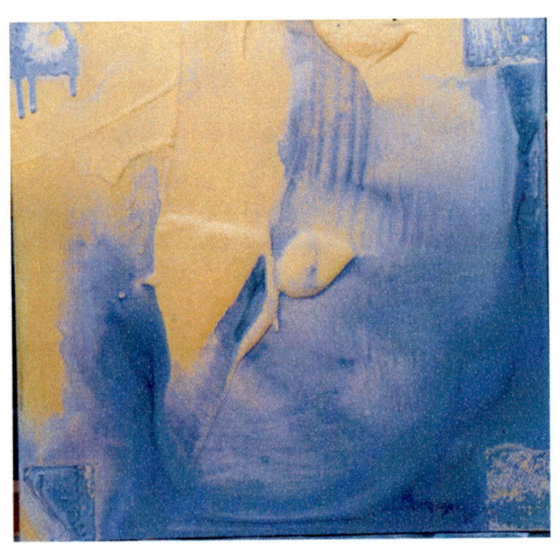

Broadway
Emulsion on panel 12 x 12″
(30 x 30cms)

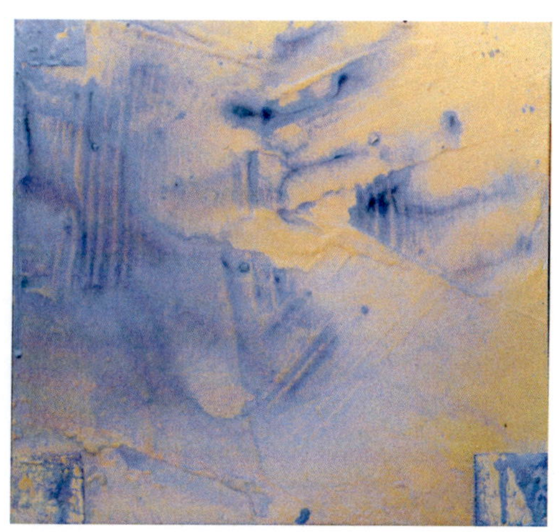

Bronx
Emulsion on panel 12 x 12"
(30 x 30cms)

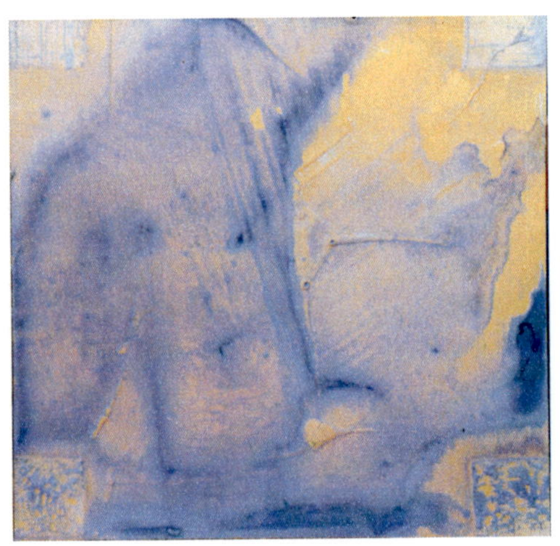

Brooklyn Heights
Emulsion on panel 12 x 12″
(30 x 30cms)

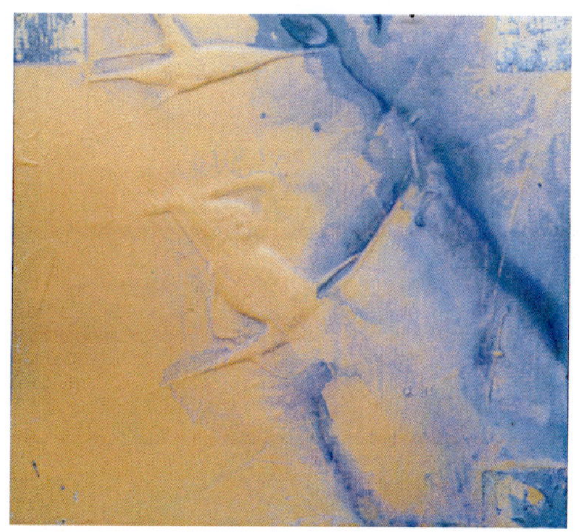

Bryant Park
Emulsion on panel 12 x 12″
(30 x 30cms)

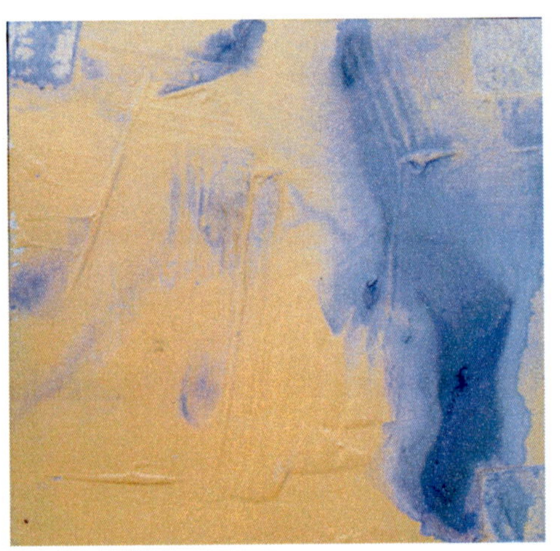

Canal Street
Emulsion on panel 12 x 12"
(30 x 30cms)

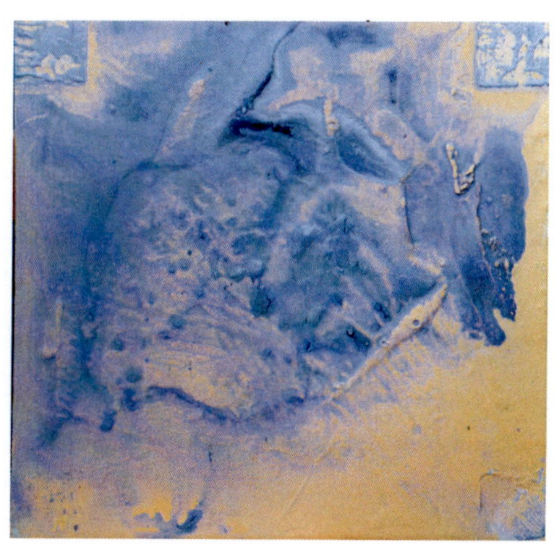

Cathedral Parkway
Emulsion on panel 12 x 12"
(30 x 30cms)

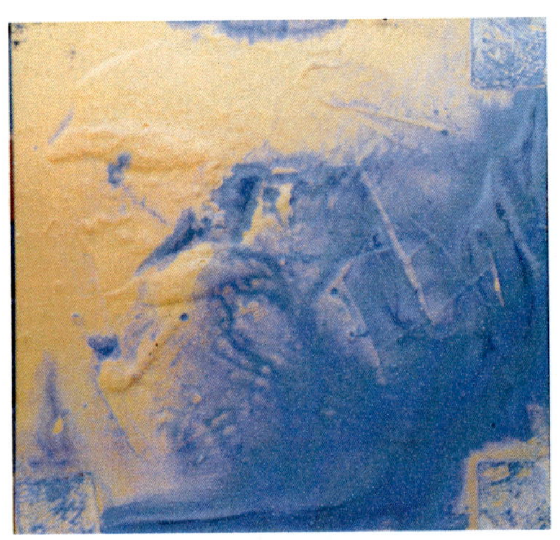

Central Park
Emulsion on panel 12 x 12"
(30 x 30cms)

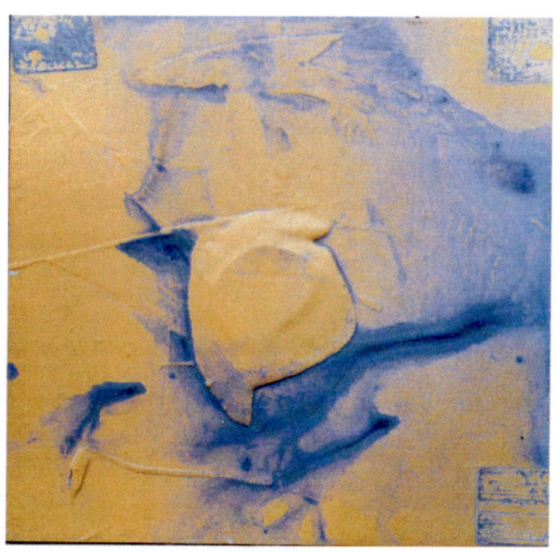

Chelsea Pier
Emulsion on panel 12 x 12″
(30 x 30cms)

24

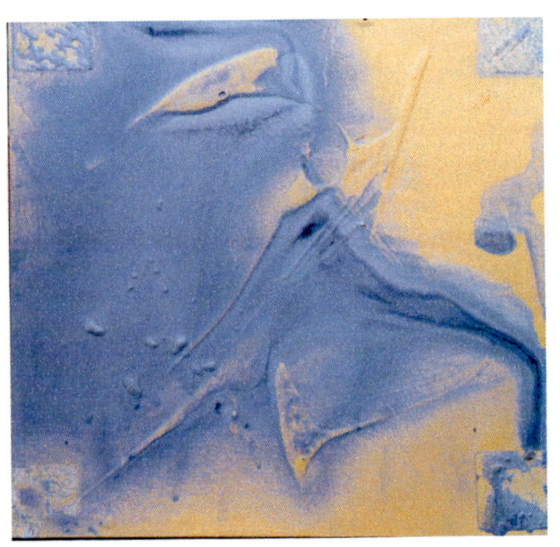

Chinatown
Emulsion on panel 12 x 12″
(30 x 30cms)

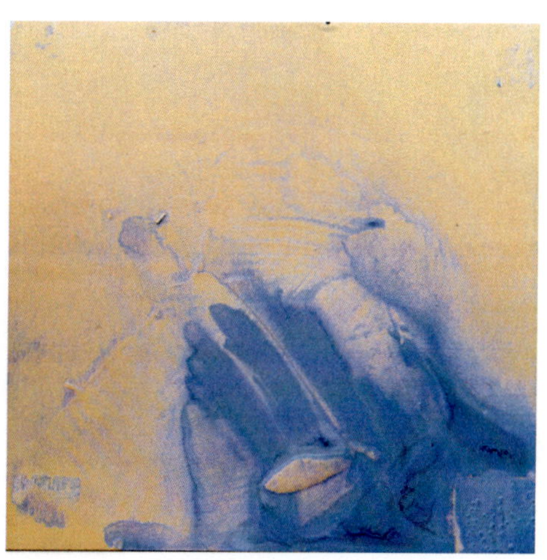

Communipaw
Emulsion on panel 12 x 12″
(30 x 30cms)

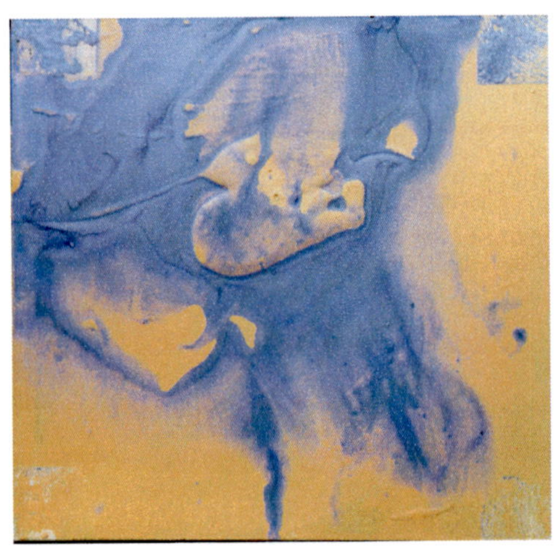

Convent Avenue
Emulsion on panel 12 x 12"
(30 x 30cms)

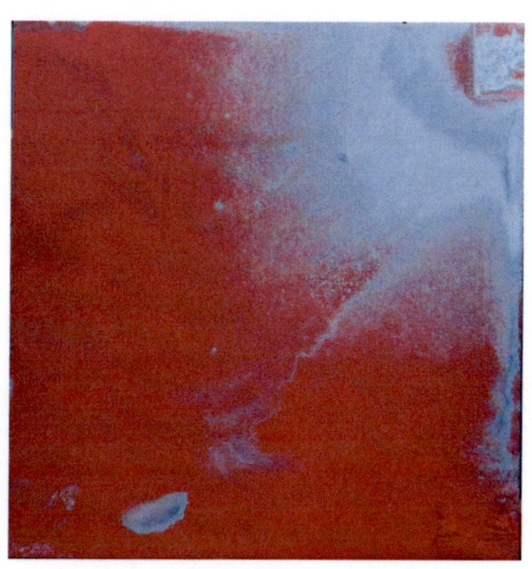

Cooper Square
Emulsion on panel 12 x 12″
(30 x 30cms)

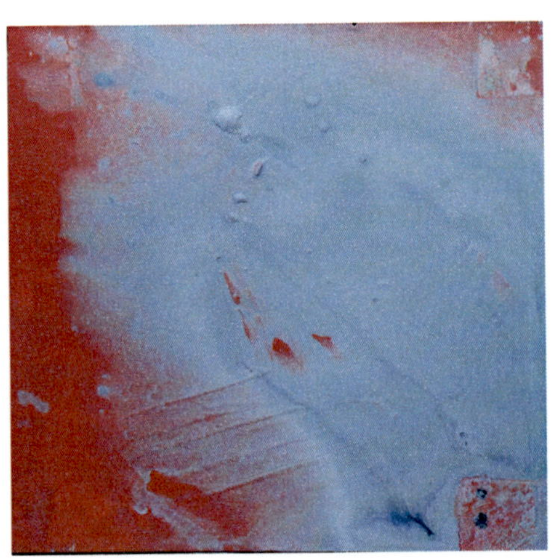

Desbrosses Street
Emulsion on panel 12 x 12″
(30 x 30cms)

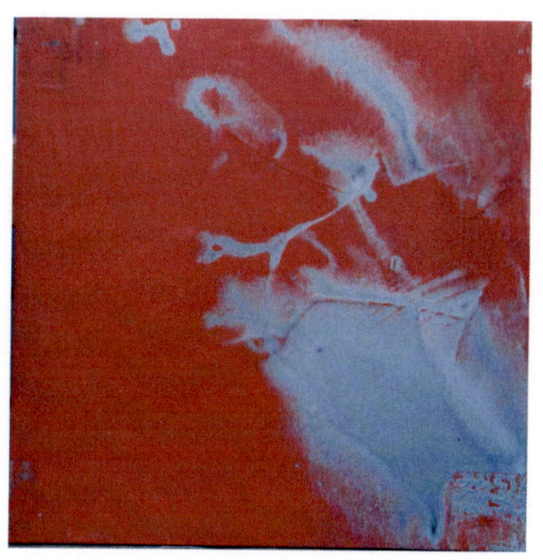

Dey Street
Emulsion on panel 12 x 12″
(30 x 30cms)

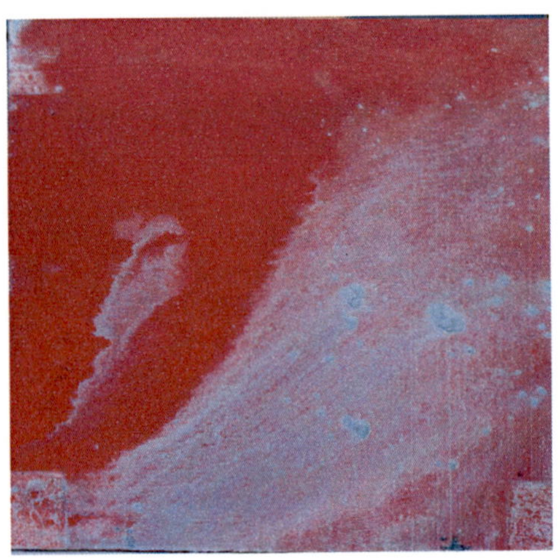

East 125th Street
Emulsion on panel 12 x 12"
(30 x 30cms)

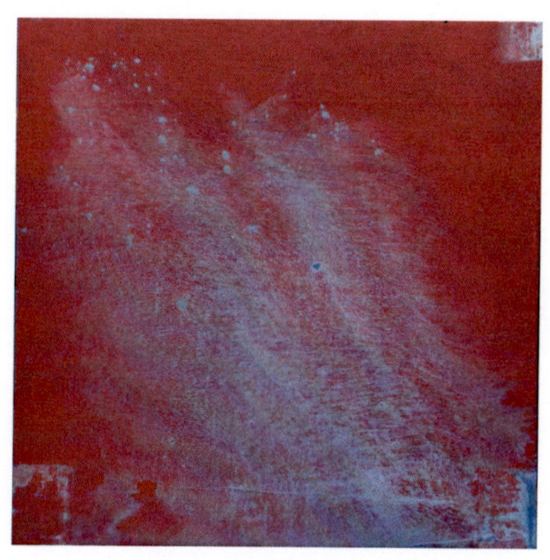

East River
Emulsion on panel 12 x 12″
(30 x 30cms)

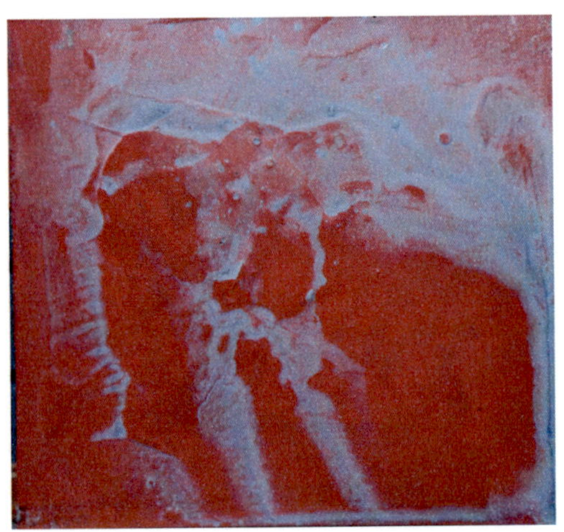

East Village
Emulsion on panel 12 x 12″
(30 x 30cms)

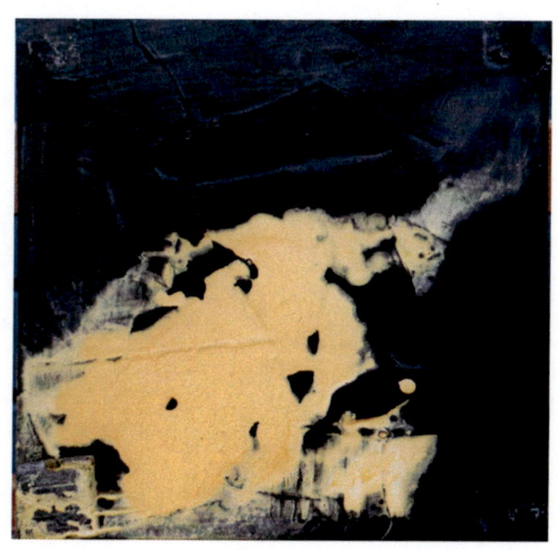

Eastern Parkway
Emulsion on panel 12 x 12″
(30 x 30cms)

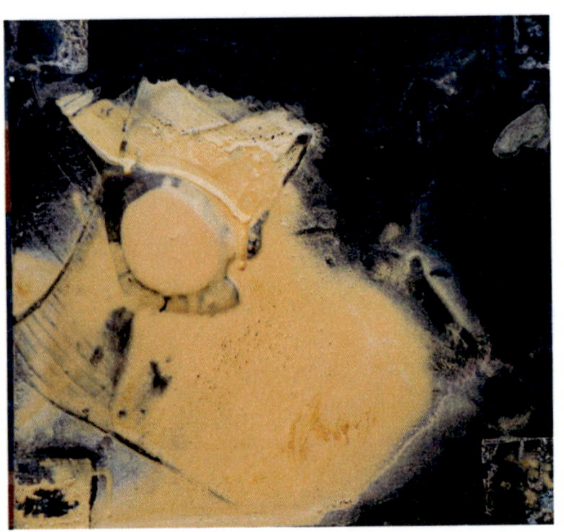

Empire State
Emulsion on panel 12 x 12"
(30 x 30cms)

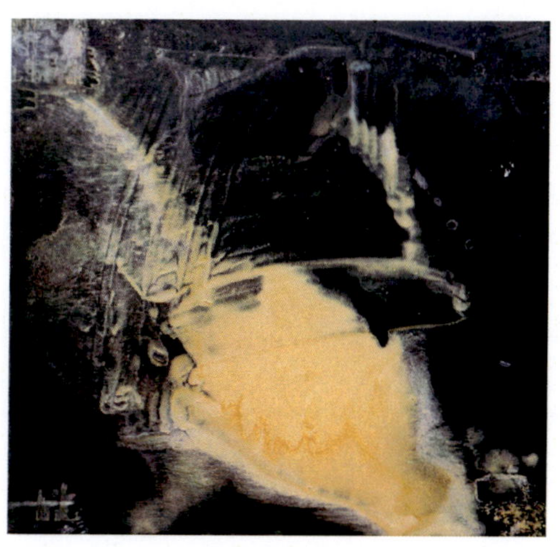

Exchange Place
Emulsion on panel 12 x 12″
(30 x 30cms)

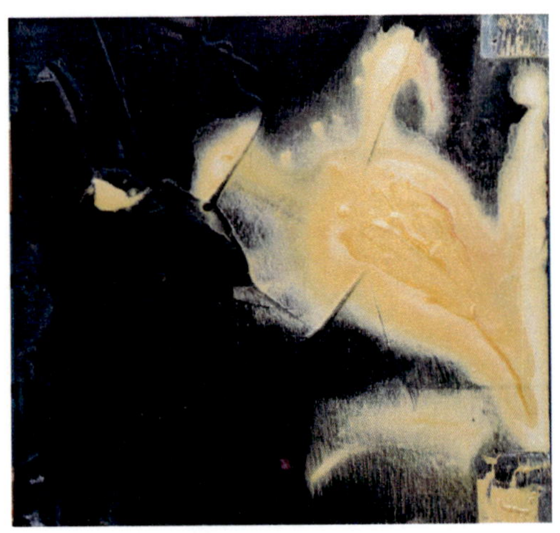

Fifth Avenue
Emulsion on panel 12 x 12"
(30 x 30cms)

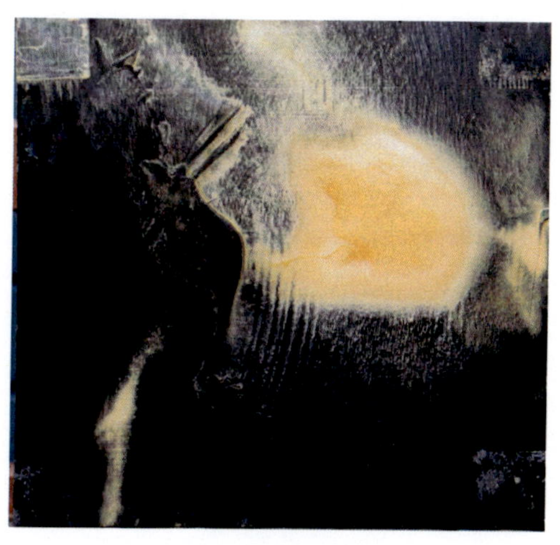

Fort Jay
Emulsion on panel 12 x 12″
(30 x 30cms)

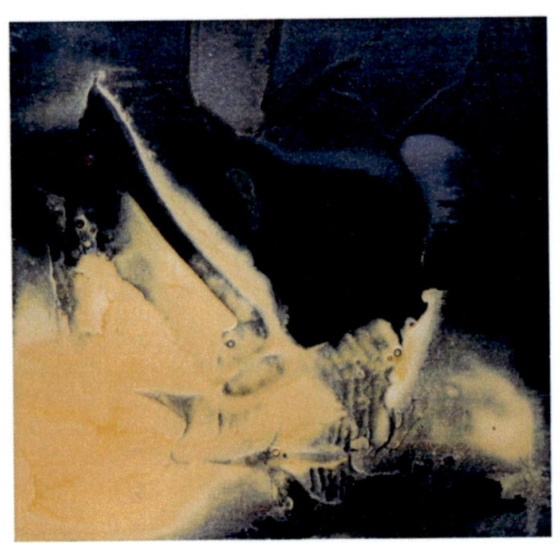

Frederick Douglas Boulevard
Emulsion on panel 12 x 12″
(30 x 30cms)

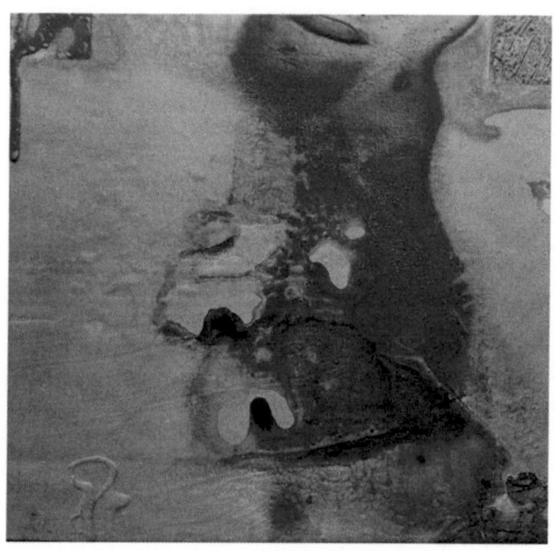

Gateway Plaza
Emulsion on panel 12 x 12″
(30 x 30cms)

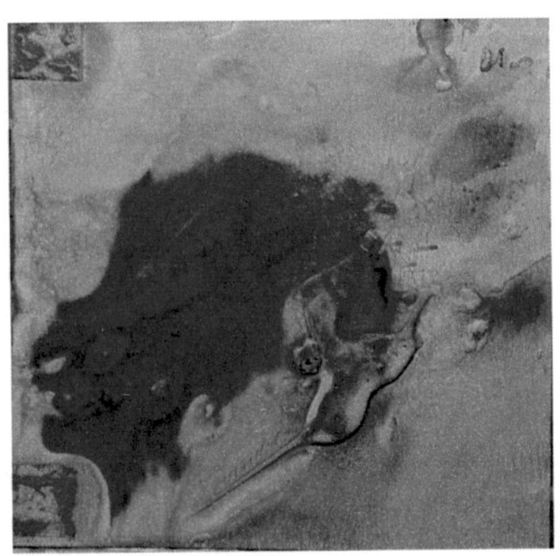

Gramercy Park
Emulsion on panel 12 x 12"
(30 x 30cms)

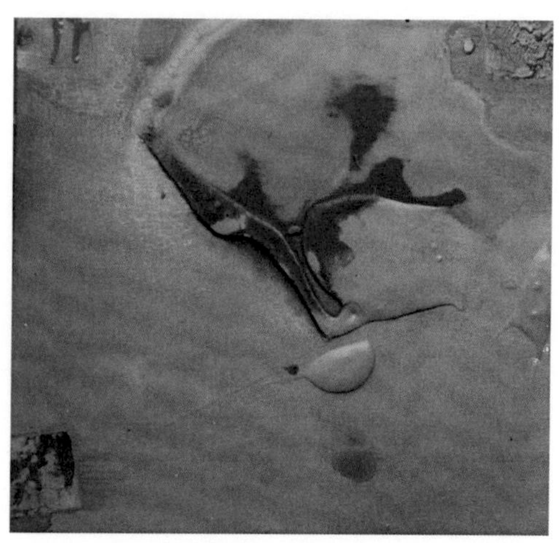

Grand Street
Emulsion on panel 12 x 12″
(30 x 30cms)

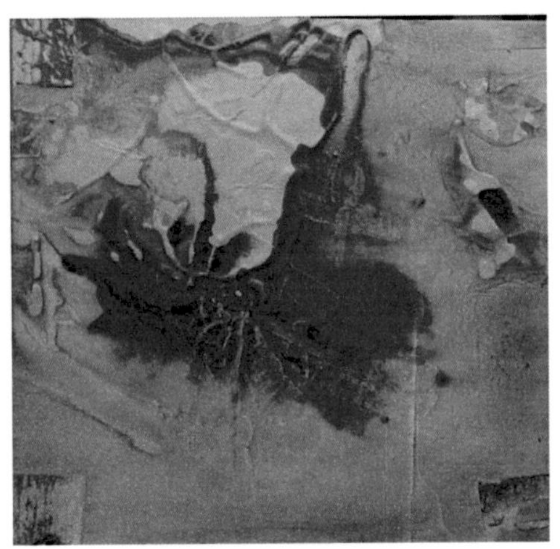

Greenwich Village
Emulsion on panel 12 x 12″
(30 x 30cms)

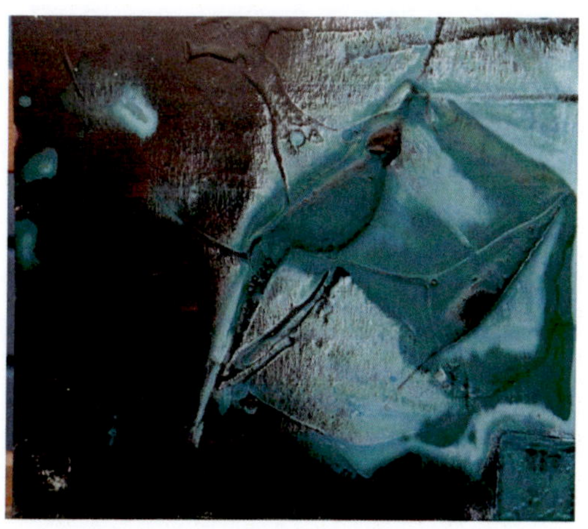

Harlem
Emulsion on panel 12 x 12″
(30 x 30cms)

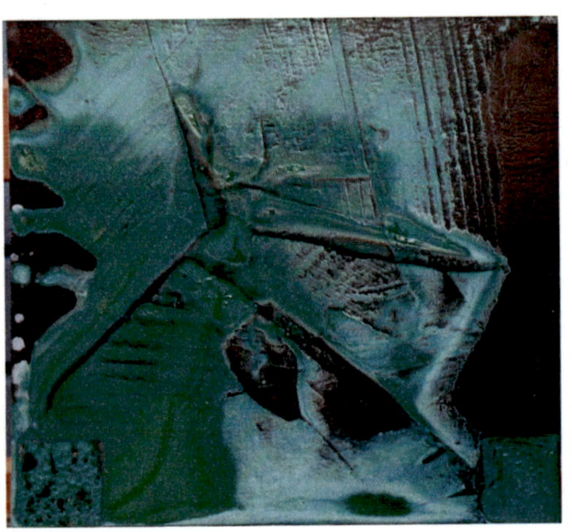

Hoboken
Emulsion on panel 12 x 12"
(30 x 30cms)

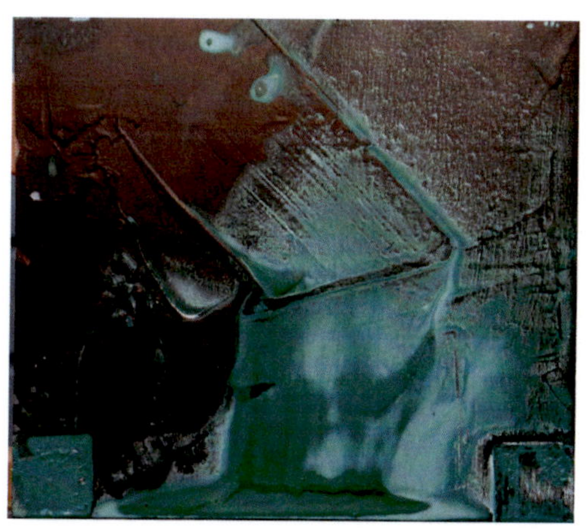

Houston Street
Emulsion on panel 12 x 12″
(30 x 30cms)

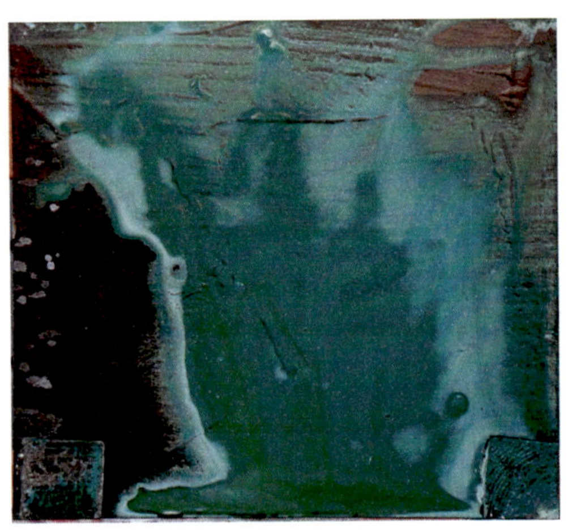

Hudson River
Emulsion on panel 12 x 12″
(30 x 30cms)

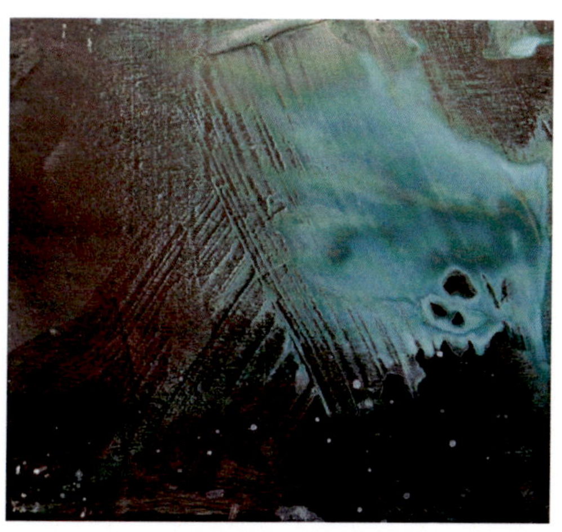

Jaqueline Kennedy Reservoir
Emulsion on panel 12 x 12″
(30 x 30cms)

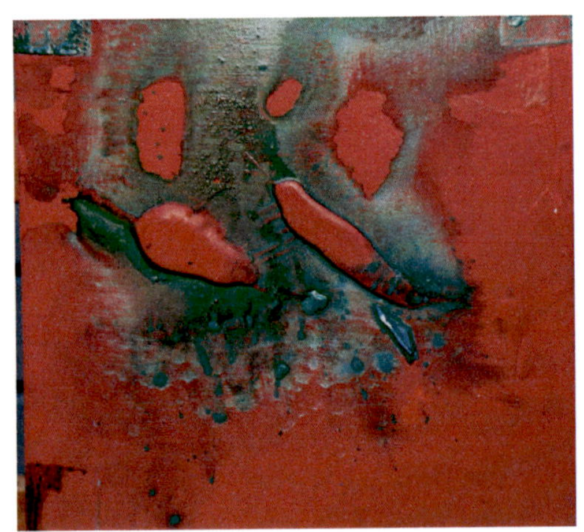

Jersey City
Emulsion on panel 12 x 12"
(30 x 30cms)

49

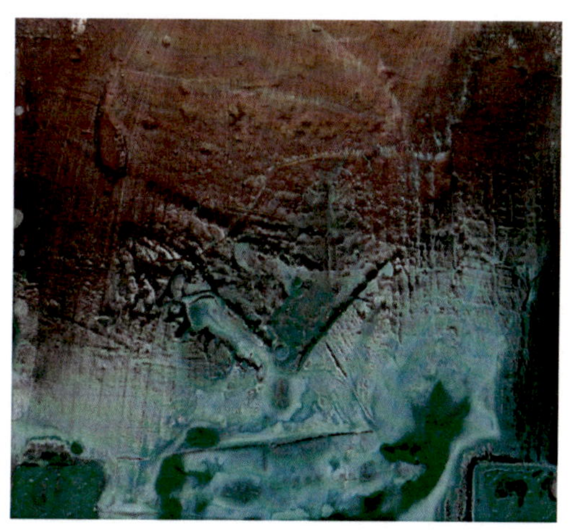

Lexington Avenue
Emulsion on panel 12 x 12″
(30 x 30cms)

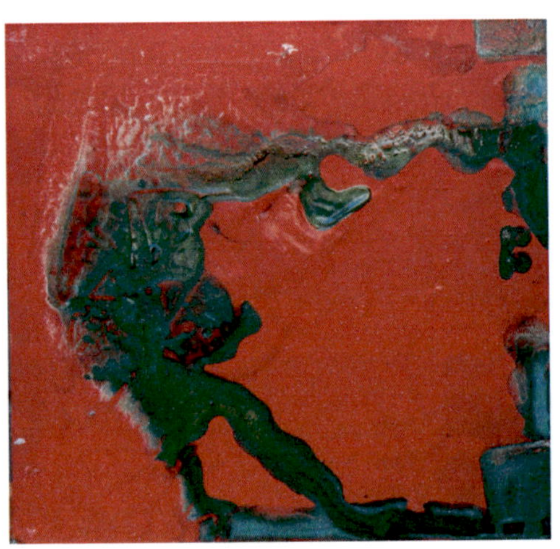

Liberty Street
Emulsion on panel 12 x 12″
(30 x 30cms)

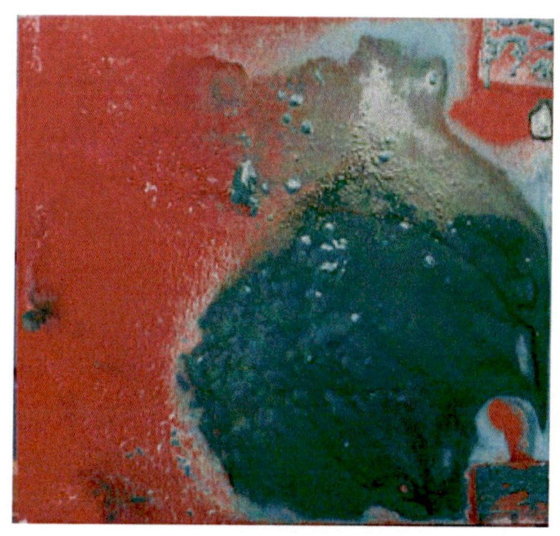

Little Italy
Emulsion on panel 12 x 12″
(30 x 30cms)

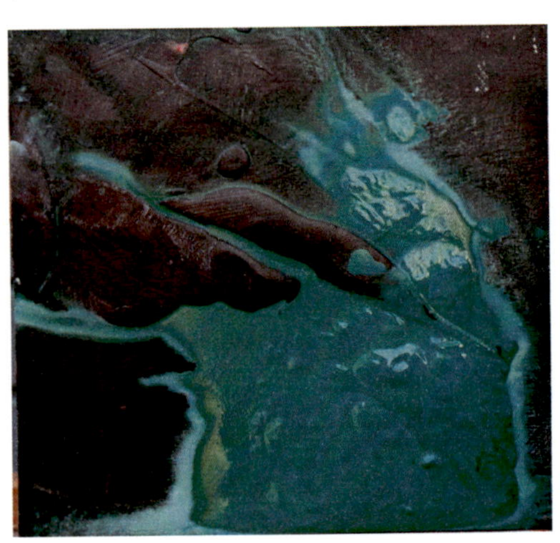

Long Isl;and City
Emulsion on panel 12 x 12″
(30 x 30cms)

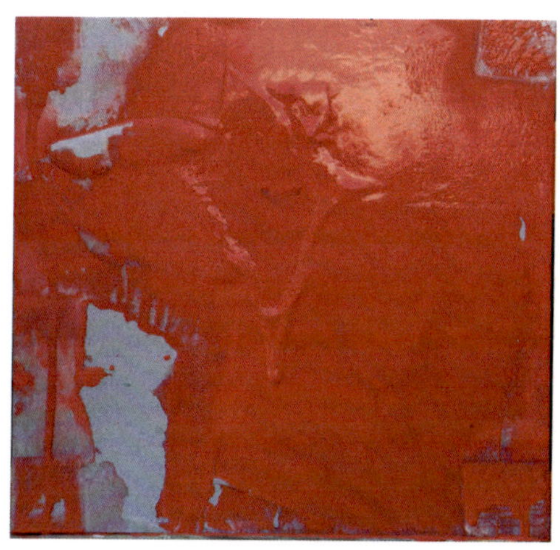

Madison Avenue
Emulsion on panel 12 x 12″
(30 x 30cms)

54

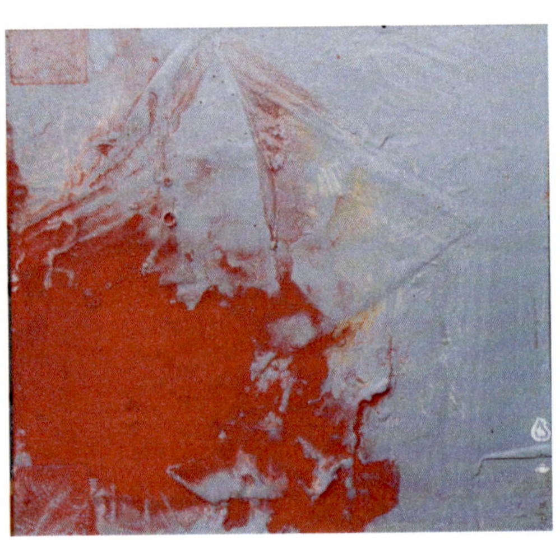

Marcus Garvey Plaza
Emulsion on panel 12 x 12″
(30 x 30cms)

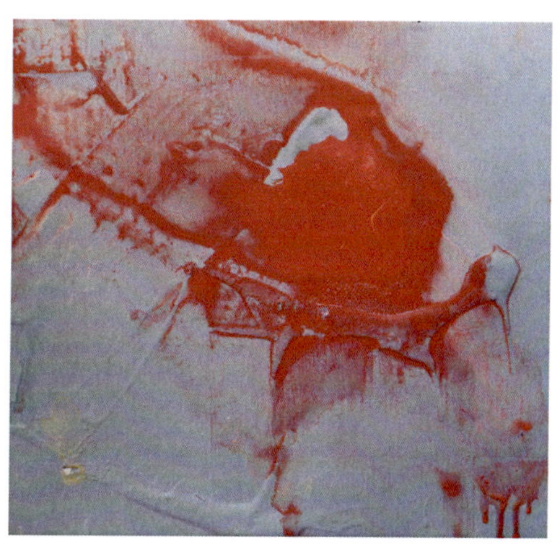

Marion
Emulsion on panel 12 x 12″
(30 x 30cms)

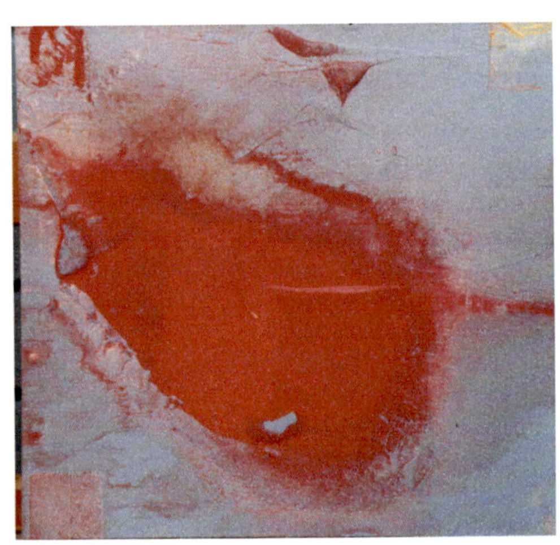

Monro Street
Emulsion on panel 12 x 12″
(30 x 30cms)

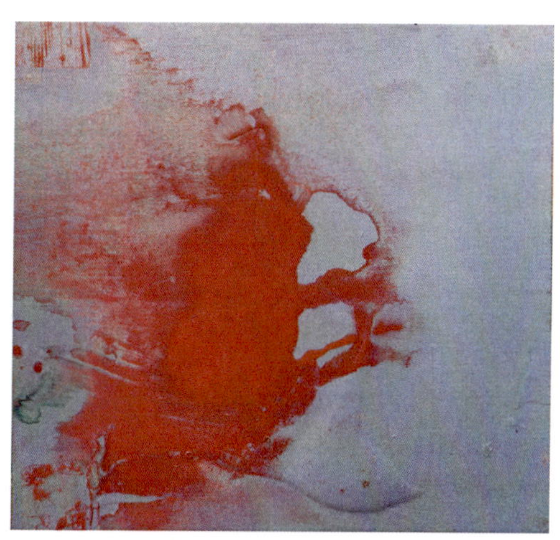

Murray Street
Emulsion on panel 12 x 12″
(30 x 30cms)

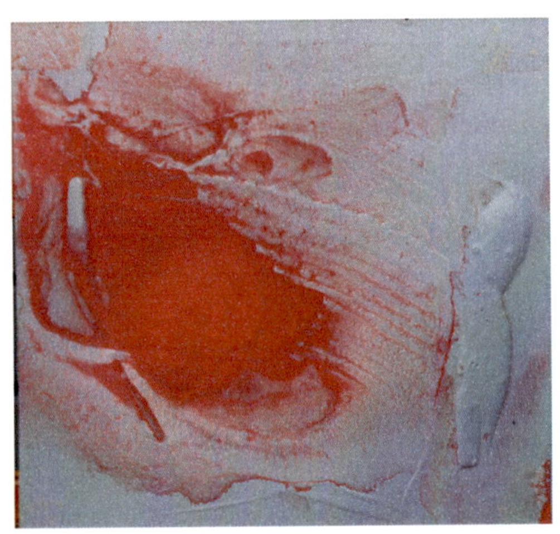

North Moore Street
Emulsion on panel 12 x 12″
(30 x 30cms)

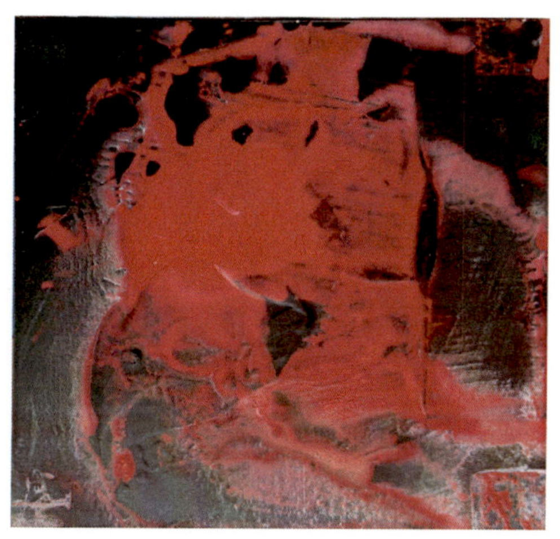

Park Avenue
Emulsion on panel 12 x 12″
(30 x 30cms)

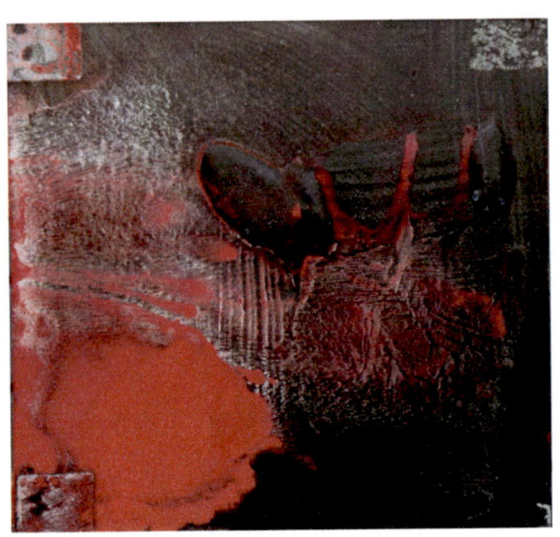

Pearl Street
Emulsion on panel 12 x 12″
(30 x 30cms)

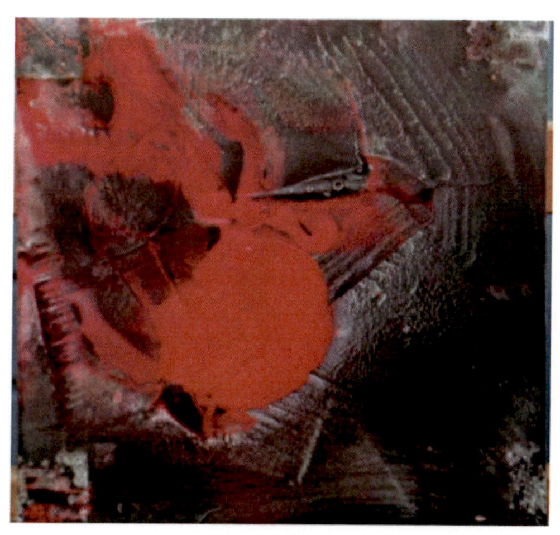

Peck Slip
Emulsion on panel 12 x 12″
(30 x 30cms)

62

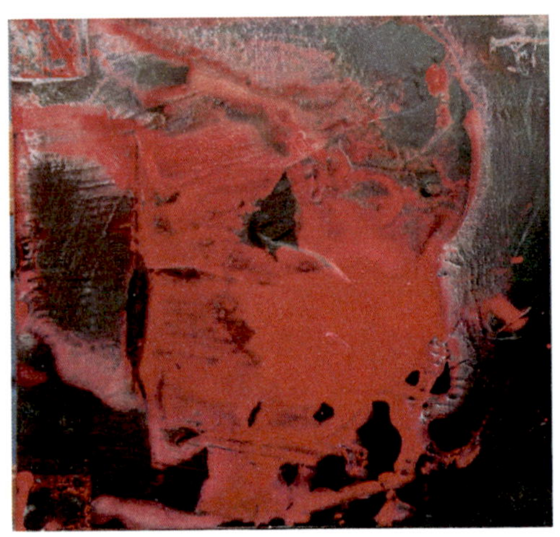

Red Hook
Emulsion on panel 12 x 12″
(30 x 30cms)

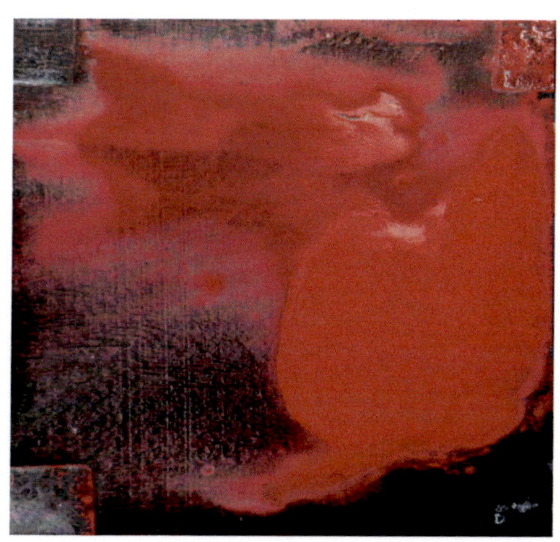

Soho Grand
Emulsion on panel 12 x 12″
(30 x 30cms)

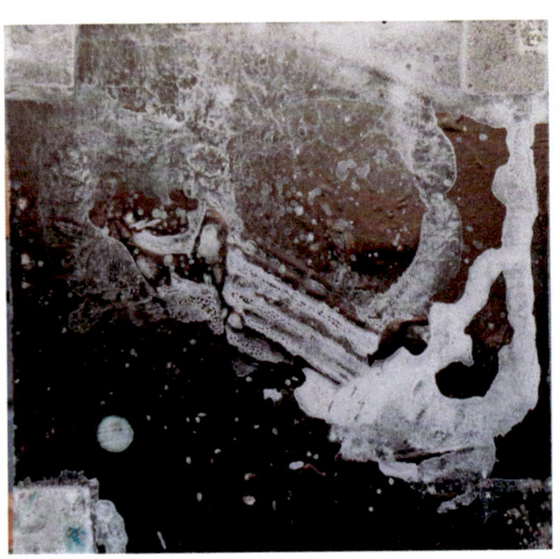

Spring Street
Emulsion on panel 12 x 12″
(30 x 30cms)

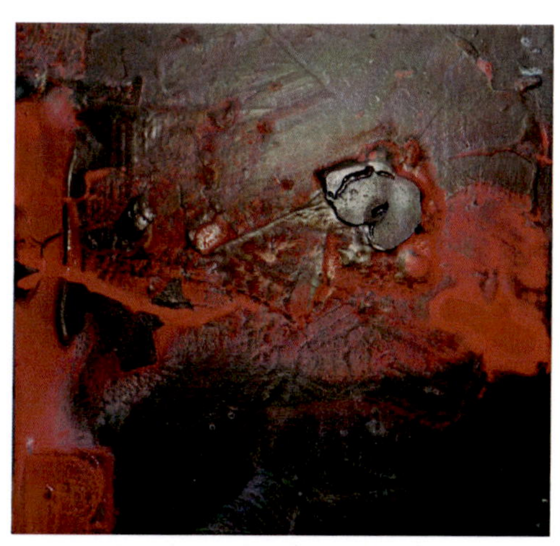

St Nicholas Park
Emulsion on panel 12 x 12″
(30 x 30cms)

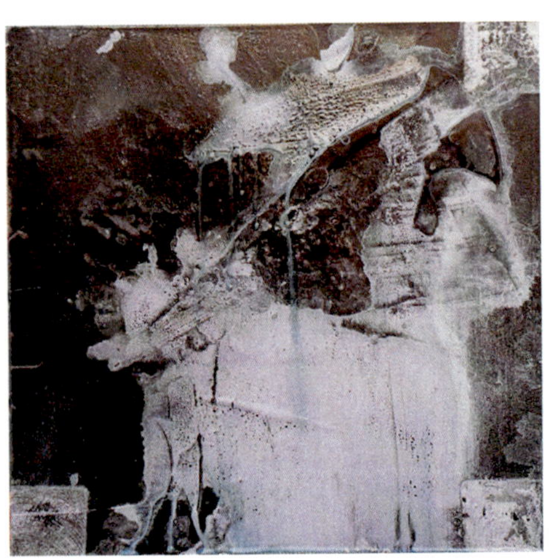

Sunnyside
Emulsion on panel 12 x 12″
(30 x 30cms)

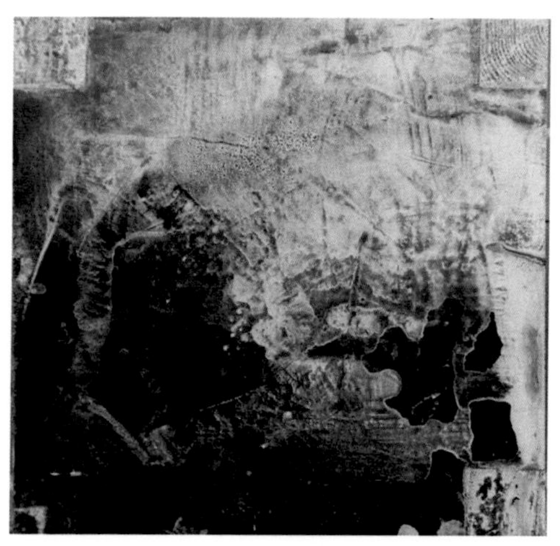

Tribeca
Emulsion on panel 12 x 12"
(30 x 30cms)

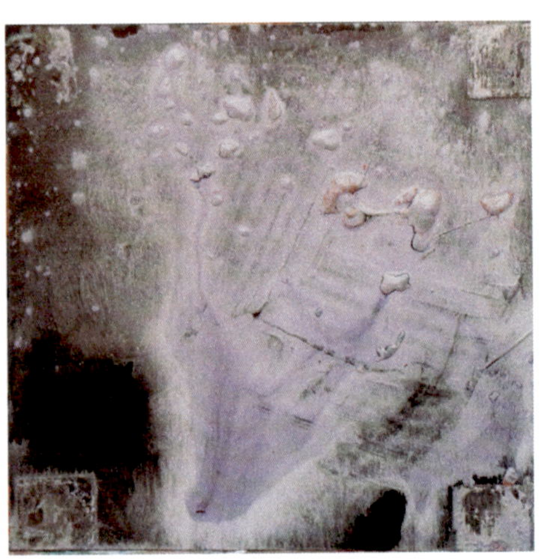

Trinity
Emulsion on panel 12 x 12″
(30 x 30cms)

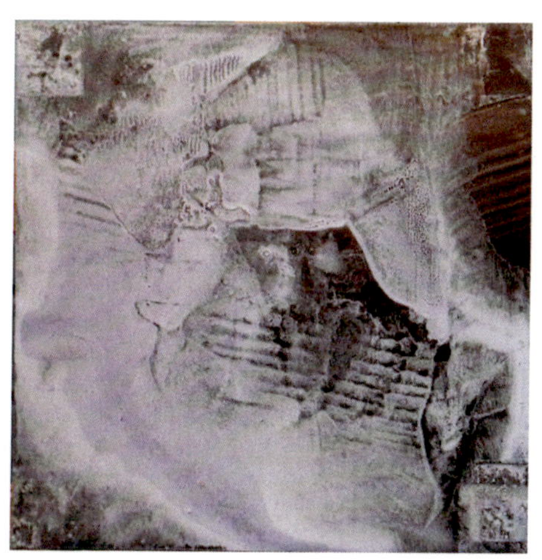

Union Square
Emulsion on panel 12 x 12"
(30 x 30cms)

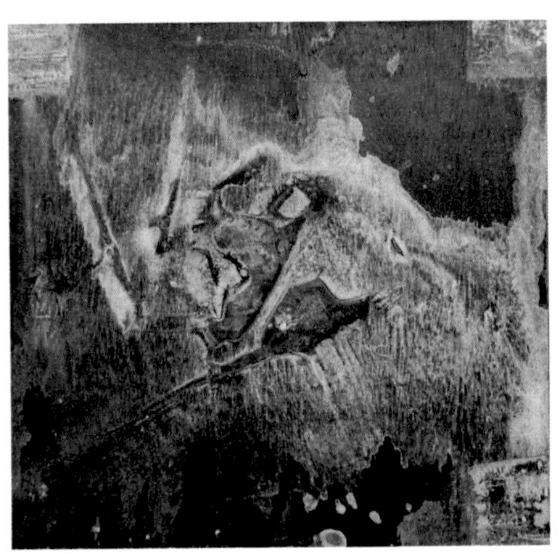

Upper New York Bay
Emulsion on panel 12 x 12"
(30 x 30cms)

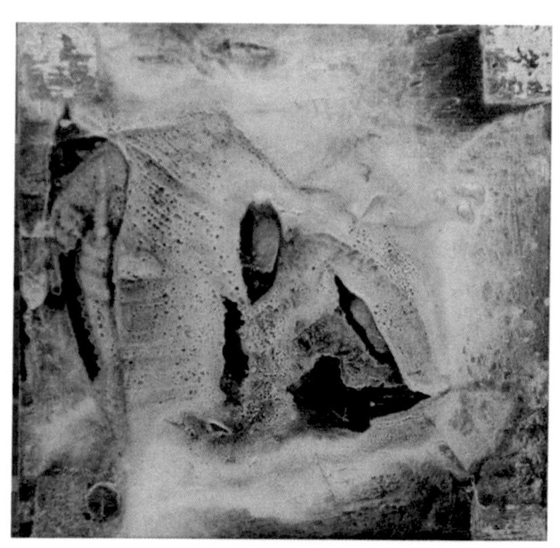

Vesey Street
Emulsion on panel 12 x 12"
(30 x 30cms)

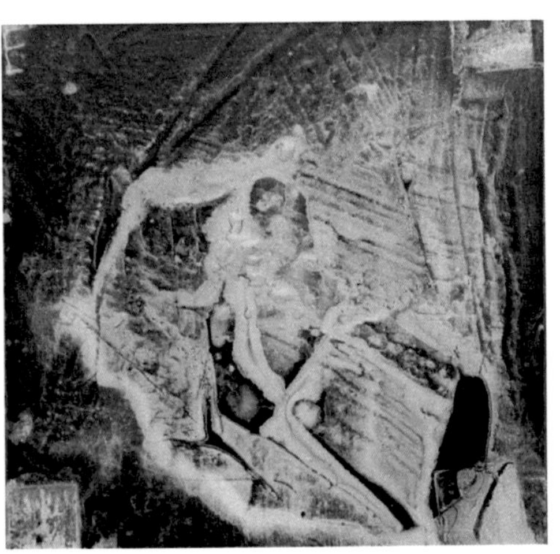

Vestrey Street
Emulsion on panel 12 x 12″
(30 x 30cms)

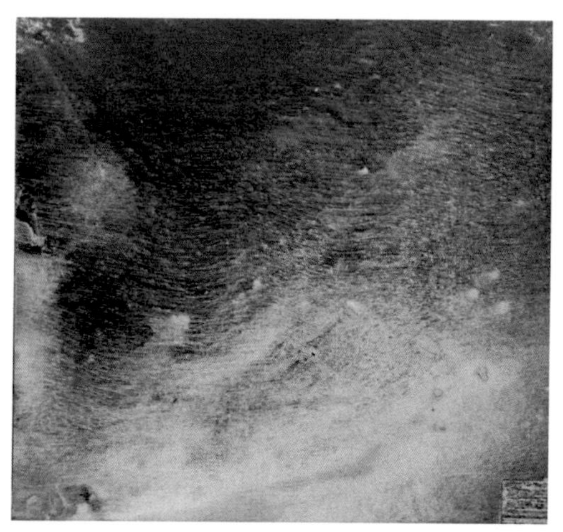

Wall Street
Emulsion on panel 12 x 12"
(30 x 30cms)

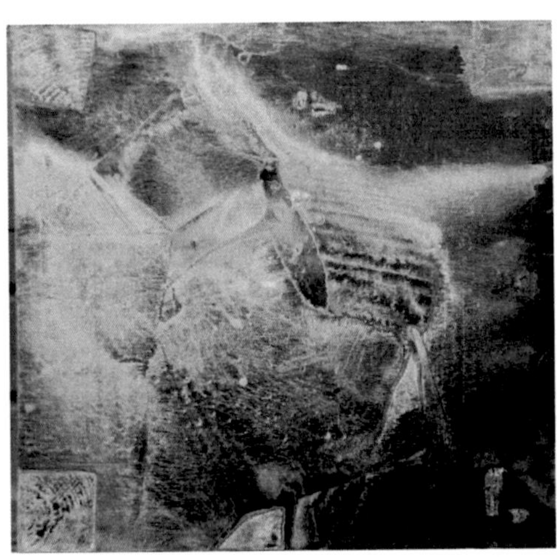

Washington Square
Emulsion on panel 12 x 12″
(30 x 30cms)

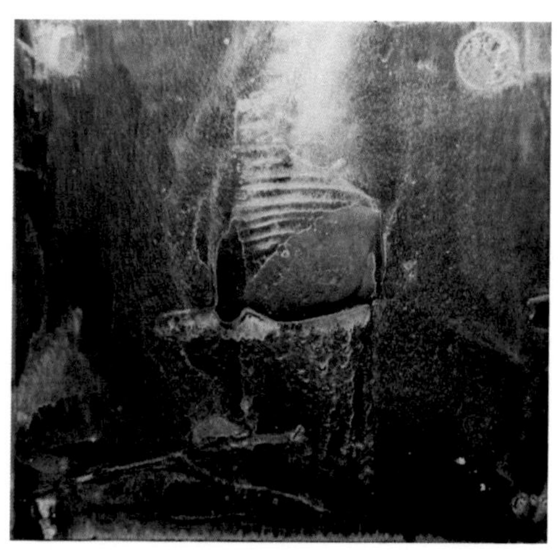

Weehawken
Emulsion on panel 12 x 12″
(30 x 30cms)

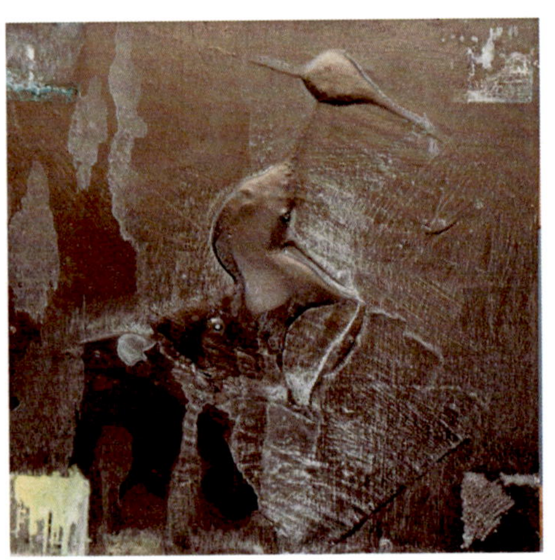

West 14th Street
Emulsion on panel 12 x 12″
(30 x 30cms)

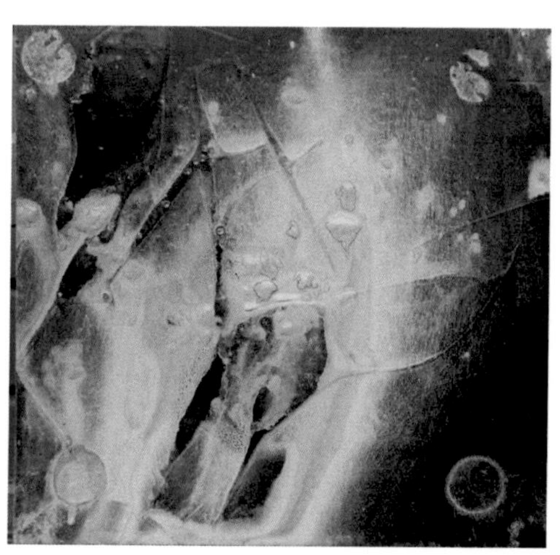

West 72nd Street
Emulsion on panel 12 x 12″
(30 x 30cms)

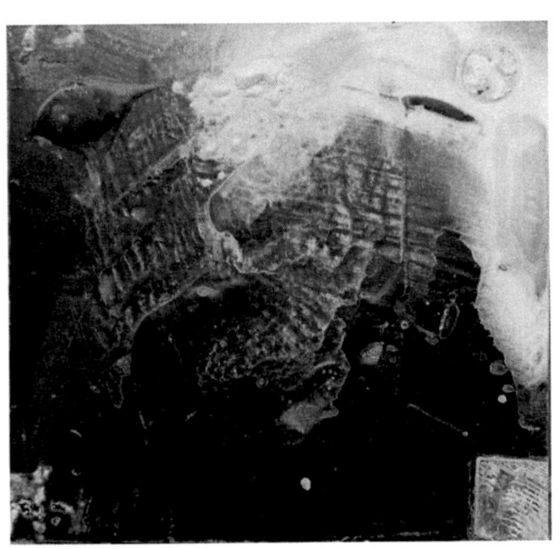

West 9th Street
Emulsion on panel 12 x 12″
(30 x 30cms)

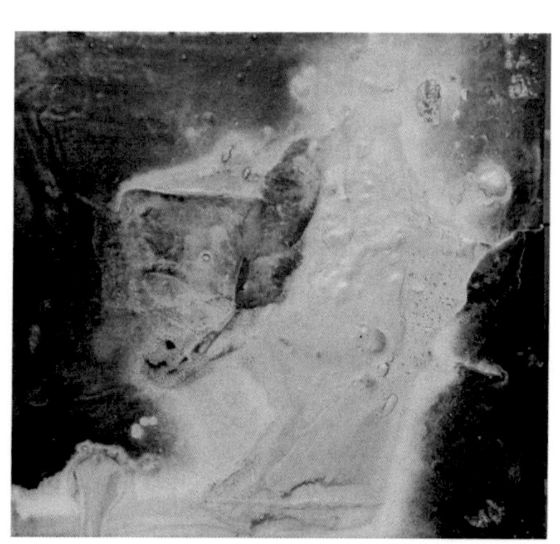

West Bergen
Emulsion on panel 12 x 12″

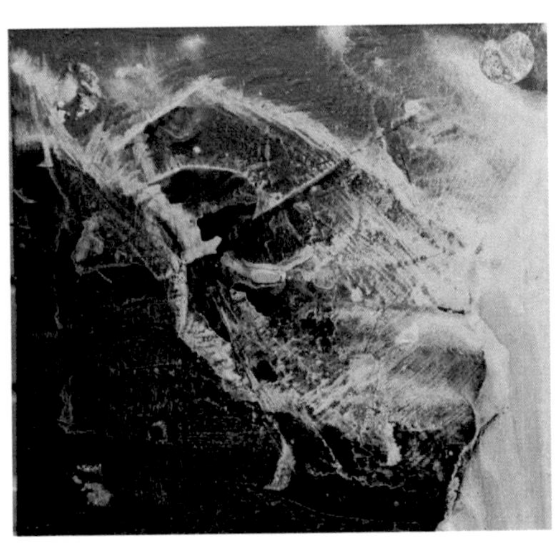

West End Avenue
Emulsion on panel 12 x 12″
(30 x 30cms)

Manhattan Notes

New York Pass
1976

1976

The George Washington Hotel

The door carries a heavy lock and chain with several bolts. "Lock it when you're inside" growls the bell boy as I offer him a dollar bill. Knife marks score the latch signifying a previous unsatisfied guest.

Kojak

"Nobody move". Searchlights strafe the hotel as police surround the building. Kojak appears on TV sucking a lollipop. The sirens of the episode blend and confuse with the blare of noise from the street.

Dime Store

A dime store on Eat 14th Street carries trays of brightly coloured bangles, brooches and pins, glass beads and accessories. The visitor reaches for some cash in his secret pocket, sewn on the inside of his jeans. "What are you doing sir?" Asks the girl behind the counter. "He's reaching for his gun" remarks her assistant drily.

Hotel Corridor

"Maybe if I hadn't been involved with..who knows" She leans against the wall in the narrow corridor of the hotel, waiting to introduce the visitor to the city.

Time Square

"You may have heard about New York City robbers" The large black man corners the terrified tourist in the shadows of Time Square. "Well I am one, and I'm going to ask you very politely for some money" He takes the one dollar bill and moves away. "There, that wasn't so bad, I was well mannered and offered you no violence".

Andy's Office

The young man in an ill-fitting suit opens large glass doors to a vacant space with polished parquet floors at 860 Broadway. He leads the visitor to the desk of the business manager. He notes the fair hair of the artist who sits with his back turned on a brown velvet drum seat, in discussion with two men in pale grey suits. A large canvas of Mao stands on two packing crates. The visitor spreads a clutch of photos for discussion and logs in his proposal. "You must meet Andy" says the manager. A moves lightly towards them, a powdered complexion masking a pitted skin. He asks what colour is this or that, turning the pictures over. "They're all black and white." Replies the visitor, somewhat embarassed. "Oh really, you must meet Victor." he says. Right on cue a skinny man with a big moustache appears from a side door. "But I the great artist Andy?" Victor Hugo says, ignoring the book. "Sure you are" Says A evenly. They offer the visitor a Friday job photographing Halston's fashion window on Fifth Avenue, then go into a private huddle signifying the end of the introduction.

Guggenheim

The long circular ramp of the Guggenheim winds up to the small room of a busy curator who leafs briefly through the show book, making pleasant non-commital remarks.

Geldzahler

Curator of the modern collection at The Metropolitan Museum Henry Geldzahler sits on a padded sofa behind a glass table with a vase of tulips. Exactly the setting of his portrait by David Hockney. "You should take a run to Philly "(Philadelphia Museum of Art Ed.) "I see what you do." He suddenly gets up and removes to a back office bringing the appointment to an abrupt close.

Modern Art Store

"Put away your cameras" The keeper of the Museum of Modern Art, Kynaston McShine instructs the guests before opening the door to the store, a cavernous space containing floor to ceiling grey metal screens on runners marked A-Z. "Which artist?" He enquires. Picasso. "Pull out P" he instructs, revealing a clutch of famous icons hooked on the mesh surface. They look at De Kooning, Warhol, Magritte and Audrey Flack, who seems to fit the ambience of the situation better than the rest.

Artforum

"But you're so young" says John Coplans, editor of Artforum Magazine, to the visitors as they discuss the result of a mutual project.

Night Bus

The night bus stops for a while, its air pressure doors flip open and a man heaves himself onto the deck, then along the gangway. He's only a torso as both legs have been amputated. A broad pool of piss spreads the sidewalk where he was waiting.

Approach

"Want a rest?" A pasty faced woman mutters to the visitor as he waits for a bus on the lower east side.

Transfers

"Where are the transfers ?" She screams as they race for a bus to cross the city. "I dropped them in a bin" He responds timidly.

Party in the Upper 80s

"Gary's from Ohio, he's studying to be a playwright." The girl with ginger hair introduces her boyfriend, a toughly built man with a firm handshake. Later on in the party she huddles in a friendly way with the English guest under the table. Her boyfriend signals her to the hallway, and a sharp crack is heard as he expresses his feelings. The next day they arrive at the hotel to say goodbye. "I'm sorry for my behaviour last night" she say, the side of her face is swollen and bruised brown. "You'd make an American" She slips in quietly before they part.

1979

The Prince George

Slanting light through the muslin curtains of The Prince George Hotel, on sheaves of posters, rugs and objects, brought over for disposal in trade fairs. "Lock your window" warns the bell boy of cat burglars who drop down from the roof." A hooker was beheaded and burnt in the next room last week" He gossips.

Harlem

"Now roll up your window and put away your camera." The graphic designer instructs as he tours his guests through Harlem, cruising slowly past groups of residents, some of whom lurch towards the car muttering messages and making gestures.

The Bronx

Split bags of refuse introduce the dank environ of 'Hell's Kitchen' in The Bronx, peeling buttressed walls situated below soaring bridges.

Park Avenue

Steam rises from vents to the subway creating the surreal atmosphere of a movie set, with the vast skyscraper blocks that line the extent of the avenue.

Charades

The gathering quickly gets into the spirit of the party with a lively enactment of charades, and all pose amiably for a group photo for the visitor's souvenir album.

1998

Hotel Marriott

A strawberry tops the tall glasses of champagne, the plates are just too small to hold the complementary starters of cheese and crackers from the buffet. But the couple sit and enjoy spectacular views of the city, seated for four hours on the slowly revolving deck of an upper floor of the Hotel Marriott in Time Square.

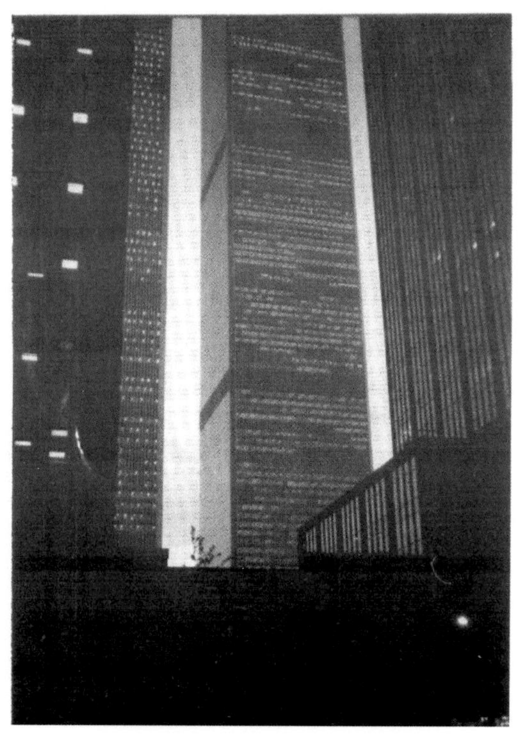

The World Trade Center from Broadway
New York May 1976

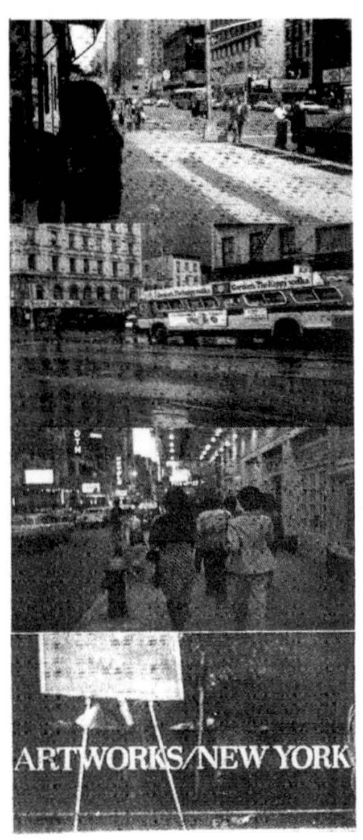

Broadway Evening, May 1976

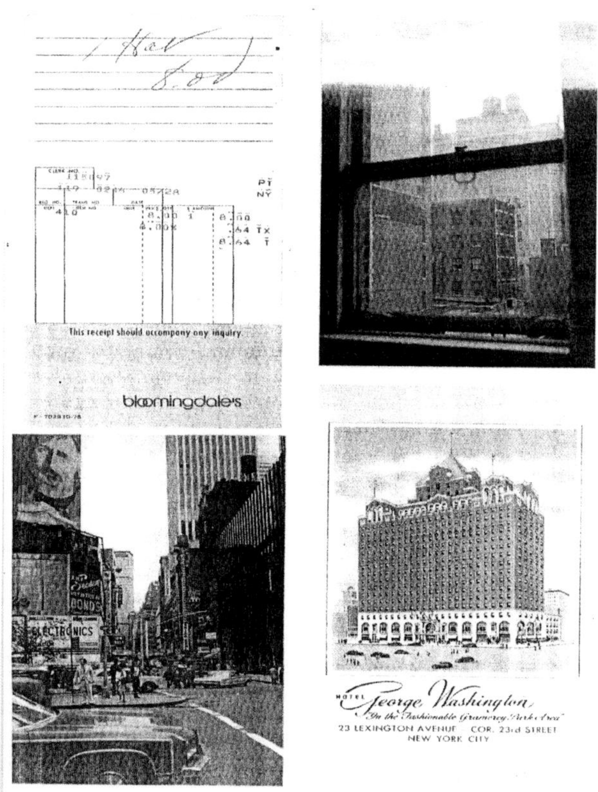

NY Receipts 1976

For catalogue information of Cv titles in print contact:
Cv Publications . The Barley Mow Centre .
10 Barley Mow Passage . London . W4 4PH UK
Tel: +44(0)20 8400 6160
www.tracksdirectory.ision.co.uk